Poems From Glamorgan

Edited by Vivien Linton

First published in Great Britain in 2010 by

 Young**Writers**

Remus House
Coltsfoot Drive
Peterborough
PE2 9JX
Telephone: 01733 890066
Website: www.youngwriters.co.uk

All Rights Reserved
Book Design by Spencer Hart
© Copyright Contributors 2009
SB ISBN 978-1-84924-762-7

Foreword

At Young Writers our defining aim is to promote an enjoyment of reading and writing amongst children and young adults. By giving aspiring poets the opportunity to see their work in print, their love of the written word as well as confidence in their own abilities has the chance to blossom.

Our latest competition Poetry Explorers was designed to introduce primary school children to the wonders of creative expression. They were given free reign to write on any theme and in any style, thus encouraging them to use and explore a variety of different poetic forms.

We are proud to present the resulting collection of regional anthologies which are an excellent showcase of young writing talent. With such a diverse range of entries received, the selection process was difficult yet very rewarding. From comical rhymes to poignant verses, there is plenty to entertain and inspire within these pages. We hope you agree that this collection bursting with imagination is one to treasure.

Contents

Cwm Glas Primary School

Greenhill Primary School

Pentrepoeth Junior School

Ysgol Mynydd Bychan

The Poems

Pain

What does it sound like?
Pain sounds like someone's laughter is being carried
Out through the wind
And being blocked out by the sound of someone crying
Because they've broken up with their best friend.

What does it feel like?
Pain feels like sadness, like your grandma or grandpa's face
Fading away into the dead of night.

What does it look like?
Pain looks like something you can never describe,
It is unique to every single person.

What colour is it?
Pain is every colour of the rainbow,
Because it can be a happy pain
(yellow, the colour of the sun),
A sad pain,
(blue, the colour of the tears that drip down your face),
A lonely pain,
(white, the colour of some deserted place),
An angry pain,
(purple, the colour of your mad, cross face),
A worried pain,
(green, the colour of your worried face),
And many, many more.

What does it smell of?
Pain can smell of anything
Like a barbecue, a hospital, or even nothing.

What does it remind you of?
Pain reminds you of someone who's gone away
And you'll never see them again.

What does it taste like?
Pain tastes like the salty water that leaks from your face.

Megan Ada Rose Forwood (9)
Bishopston Primary School

Happiness

What does it taste of?
Happiness tastes like an everlasting ice cream
Of all different flavours.
What does it smell like?
Happiness smells like my dad's aftershave
When we go out to family dinners.
What does it look like?
Happiness looks like people on surfboards
Driving in the deep sea waves.
What does it feel like?
Happiness feels like a dream come true,
When I fly through space and take a step on the moon.
What does it remind me of?
Happiness reminds me of elephants stomping around
In circles under a colourful sunset.
What does it sound like?
Happiness sounds like a school bell ringing
And children screaming.
What colour is it?
Happiness is multicoloured because everything I do
Has some
Happiness!

Maryanne Eve (10)
Bishopston Primary School

Fear

Fear is a great white shark lurking through the ocean.
Fear is a lion pouncing on its prey.
Fear is black, like the dark night around you.
Fear is like a snake slithering through the sand.
We are all scared of different things,
But that does not make them scary,
It is what we choose that makes them scary.
Fear is undefined . . .

Hannah Morgan (10)
Bishopston Primary School

Silence

What colour is it?
Silence is black, the colour of stillness, calmness and peace.
What does it remind you of?
Silence reminds me of sadness, happiness, adventure,
Fearful moments and fearsome films.
What does it smell of?
Silence smells of the robins singing gently to the falling of snow
                                    at the beginning of Christmas.
What does it taste of?
Silence tastes of a picnic all alone in the mountains of west Wales.
What does it feel like?
Silence feels like walking through a cloud with no breeze.
A bird singing a song that nobody has heard of before,
                                            but recognises.
What does it sound like?
Silence sounds like a black cave echoing through the darkness,
But all I hear is the rocks falling down in the distance.
What does it look like?
Silence looks like trees stood close together
And vines growing out of the bushes,
It looks like tigers roaming through the jungle.

Eleanor Pearce
Bishopston Primary School

Love

What colour is it?
Love is the colour of a cherry freshly picked from a tree.
Love smells of roses still on their stalk.
What does it sound like?
It sounds like two people dancing all night!
What does it taste like?
It tastes like chocolate that has been made.
What does it look like?
Two people looking at each other.

Olivia Monks (9)
Bishopston Primary School

3

Love

What does love smell of?
Love smells like a fresh smell of flowers
Blowing in the glowing autumn breeze.
What does love feel like?
Love feels like a heart of love
Pumping beautiful feelings around your body.
What does love look like?
Love looks like a bride in a beautiful white gown
Blowing in the golden sun.
What colour is love?
Love is a deep red, like beautiful red roses
With petals falling off, one by one.
What does love taste of?
Love tastes of beautiful textures
Of creamy bonbons melting in your mouth.
What does love remind you of?
Love reminds me of my mum's
Home-made chocolate cake and delicate daisies.
What does love sound like?
Love sounds like the wonderful sound of crashing waves.

Megan E Wilkes (10)
Bishopston Primary School

Sadness

Sadness is the colour of the grey clouds floating by on an
                                                autumn day.
Sadness smells like the fumes from a car as it sets off in the
                                                early morning.
Sadness sounds like a homeless child crying for help.
Sadness tastes like the salt of the sea as it touches your lips.
Sadness looks like an open forest as you are about to step into it.
Sadness feels like the waves as they crash through you.
Sadness reminds me of the bad dreams I have in the
                                pitch-blackness of the night.

Juno Harley Davies (9)
Bishopston Primary School

4

Fun

What does it taste like?
Fun tastes like candyfloss
Melting in your mouth on a summer holiday.
What does it sound like?
Fun sounds like people having fun at the beach.
What colour is it?
Fun is blue like having fun in the swimming pool.
What does it remind you of?
Fun reminds me of me and Grandad making rope swings
Down in the forest on a hot summer's day.
What does it look like?
Fun looks like people down at the beach
Playing on a summer day.
What does it smell of?
Fun smells of all my friends
Coming over and having a barbecue.
What does it feel like?
Fun feels like when I go to the park
And go on the monkey bars on a hot summer day.

Connor Holt (11)
Bishopston Primary School

Fear

Fear is black like a ninja's costume.
It feels like you're about to fall off the cliff.
Fear sounds like the waves crashing against rocks.
Fear is the sound of wind.
Fear tastes like something you hate,
Something like mouldy cheese or gone-off milk.
Fear smells like the stench of sewers,
And the smell of socks when you wear them for over a year.
Fear looks like a man burning in flames.
Fear reminds me of things that are scary,
Like walking over a bridge that's 700 feet high and 50 feet long.

Harry Silvey (10)
Bishopston Primary School

Silence

What does it look like?
Silence looks like calm clouds after a thunderstorm.
What does it smell of?
Silence smells of a fresh fall of snow.
What does it taste like?
Silence tastes like a breath of quietness
In a calm room with nobody to see.
What colour is it?
Silence is black, like a dark night
As quietness turns into darkness with an overcast sky.
What does it feel like?
Silence feels like a touch of softness
As everything gets quieter.
What does it remind you of?
Silence reminds me of me and my family
Relaxing on the beach.
What does it sound like?
Silence sounds like the end of time,
As if nothing is going on.

Asher Fisher (10)
Bishopston Primary School

Fun

What colour is it?
Fun is multicoloured, just like a rainbow.
What does it smell of?
Fun smells of new cut grass in the summer,
When children play and have fun.
What does it sound like?
Fun sounds like the sound of the waves at the beach.
What does it taste like?
Fun tastes like eating sweets when you come home from school.
What does it look like?
Fun looks like water splashing on the beach on a windy day.

Megan Gibbon (10)
Bishopston Primary School

Sadness

What does it sound like?
Like peace throughout the world
When it isn't.
What does it feel like?
Like a salty waterfall of sobs
Splashing around inside you.
What does it taste like?
Like a bitter lemon sea,
Flowing down your throat.
What does it remind you of?
Sadness reminds me of
The grey clouds that pass above.
What colour is it?
A bluey-grey like a cold, cloudy sky.
What does it look like?
Like people ignoring each other and saying mean things.
What does it smell like?
Like a flower dying that has just come out.

Alys Dow (9)
Bishopston Primary School

Senses Changing

Sadness is black, like lonely shadows,
Joy is red, like tomatoes in a salad,
Sadness is grey, like clouds full of rain,
Joy is yellow, like the scorching sun,
Sadness is brown, like planes bombing in the war,
Joy is smiles, like the colours of the rainbow,
Sadness reminds me of horrible things,
Joy reminds me of children playing in the street,
Sadness is mean, mean to me,
Joy is happy, running through the waves,
Senses are different, changing life
Changing how we feel day and night.

Anna Rees (10)
Bishopston Primary School

Fun

What does it remind you of?
Fun reminds me of riding my pony
Along the beach at 7 o'clock
When the waves are calm and there is not a soul on the beach.
What does it taste like?
Fun tastes like a zingy bag of sherbet.
What does it smell of?
Fun smells of newly cut grass on a summer's day.
What does it look like?
Fun looks like children running around and having fun.
What does it feel like?
Fun feels like the golden sun
Shining on your cheeks as you play.
What colour is it?
The colour of fun is multicoloured
Because everything I do is fun.
What does it sound like?
Fun sounds like children screaming with glee as they play.

Jessica Walter (10)
Bishopston Primary School

Pain

Pain is blue, like the ocean and the sea.
Pain is red, like the blood inside your body.
Pain feels like the end of the world,
For it makes the tears fall down from your eyes.
It puts you in misery until you are lifted out of the pain.
It smells like you are about to meet your doom.
It feels like you have nothing.
No home, no bed, no toys, no family.
Pain.

Lowri Beth Ratti (10)
Bishopston Primary School

Silence

What colour is it?
Silence is the colour of the blue sea,
Completely motionless and calm.
What does it sound like?
Silence sounds like the end of time
Where there is nothing to be heard for hundreds of miles.
What does it remind me of?
Silence reminds me of the darkness of the night
When all you can hear is the hoot of an owl.
What does it taste of?
Silence tastes of the air when a breeze is blowing in your face.
What does it feel like?
Silence feels like the cool of the evening
After a long summer day.
What does it smell of?
Silence smells of a musty library that has long been forgotten.
What does it look like?
Silence looks like the face of a golden child, fast asleep.

Ianto Griffin (10)
Bishopston Primary School

Fear

Fear is red and it pulls tight inside you.
Fear is black, closing up around you.
Fear is blue like waves pulling you down.
It curls up in your body.
Fear is cold and makes you feel weak inside.
It smells fresh.
It's blank and cold.
And you feel like you are stuck with nowhere to go.
Then it becomes yellow as the hole opens.

Cai Adams (11)
Bishopston Primary School

Joy

What colour is it?
Joy is gold, like the sun glittering in the sky.
What does it feel like?
Joy feels like the waves crashing on your head.
What does it look like?
Joy looks like a sunflower bathing in the sun.
What does it sound like?
Joy sounds like children laughing
As they play in the snow.
What does it remind you of?
Joy reminds me of playing in the sea
On a fine summer's day.
What does it taste of?
Joy tastes of ice cream cooling you down
As it runs down your throat.
What does it smell like?
Joy smells like roast dinner
At the end of a long summer's day.

Jack Jones (10)
Bishopston Primary School

Fame

Fame is golden, like a superstar,
Fame is a silver star shining in the sky,
Fame is that wonderful, warm feeling inside you,
Fame is what keeps your heart going,
Fame is something you don't want to lose
But don't let fame go before friends and family,
Otherwise you'll lose them and fame becomes nothing.

Lorna Edwards (10)
Bishopston Primary School

Fun

What does it remind you of?
Fun reminds me of the light
That spreads through the branches of a tree in the distance.
What colour is it?
Yellow is the colour of fun, it's like a yellow sunflower
Blowing in the fun and warm breeze.
What does it smell like?
It smells like the morning dew when you wake up
In your pyjamas and open your bedroom window.
What does it look like?
It looks like a seed that has grown into a tree.
What does it sound like?
It sounds like a bluebird chirping and flying past the sun.
What does it taste like?
It tastes like a popping spark in your mouth.
What does it feel like?
It feels like a step that pushes you into a leap!

Rhiannydd Burn-Andrews (9)
Bishopston Primary School

Fun

What does it smell of?
Fun smells like you're in a field filled with roses.
What does it feel like?
Fun feels like you're on a swing swinging to and fro.
What colour is it?
It is the colour of the sea.
It is blue like swimming with the fish.
What does it remind me of?
It reminds me of my family when we were all playing together.
What does it taste like?
It tastes like hot chocolate running down your throat.
What does it look like?
It looks like playing with your friends in the park.

Meghan Vonk (10)
Bishopston Primary School

Fun

What colour is it?
Playing in a fun room full of my best friends and going down
a multicoloured slide and landing in a big pit of small balls.
What does it smell of?
It smells of sweets, squash, food and drinks.
What does it sound like?
It sounds like getting a strike in bowling.
What does it taste like?
Fun tastes like having pizza every day.
What does it look like?
A multi-coloured indoor park with activities all around it.
What does it feel like?
Fun feels like playing outside school, and playing with your
friends on a football pitch.
What does it remind you of?
It reminds me of going to a park outside and breathing in the
fresh air.

Cellan Pitson (9)
Bishopston Primary School

Joy

What colour is it?
Joy is the colour of pink, like a pink cake on my birthday.
What does joy feel like?
Joy feels like my best friend hugging me when I fall over.
What does it smell of?
Joy smells like ice cream when the ice cream van comes.
What does it sound like?
Joy sounds like the cry of a new baby being born.
What does it taste like?
Joy tastes like when my mum kisses me.
What does it look like?
Joy looks like a big swimming pool, waiting to be jumped in.
Joy reminds me of when I get a new puppy.

Emily Jones (8)
Bishopston Primary School

Happiness

What does it taste like?
Happiness tastes of fluffy pink candyfloss.
What does it smell of?
Happiness smells of a pizza, coming out of an oven.
What does it look like?
Happiness looks like a child, full of fun.
What colour is it?
Happiness is the colour of yellow,
As the sun shines upon your face.
What does it feel like?
Happiness feels like a great, huge smile across your face.
What does it remind you of?
Happiness reminds me of children, playing in the fields.
What does it sound like?
Happiness sounds like children,
Splashing about in a huge, glistening pool.

Kaela Thompson (10)
Bishopston Primary School

Fun

What does it taste like?
Fun tastes like candyfloss in your mouth
On a summer's day at the fair.
What does it look like?
Fun looks like a person going down a water slide
And getting a wedgie.
What does it smell like?
Fun smells of chestnuts being roasted in the evening.
What does it feel like?
Fun feels like running a race on sports day.
What colour is it?
Fun is pink, the colour of a sunset on an autumn evening.
What does it remind you of?
Fun reminds me of going down a water slide.

Oscar Ley (10)
Bishopston Primary School

Fun

What does it taste like?
Fun tastes like ice cream melting in my mouth.
What colour is it?
The colour of fun is the green grass beneath my feet when I'm
                                        playing football.
What does it sound like?
Fun sounds like the waves crashing on the sand.
What does it smell of?
Fun smells like a brand new summer's day.
What does it feel like?
Fun feels like a new football in my hands.
What does it remind you of?
Fun reminds me of playing with my friends.
What does it look like?
Fun looks like children playing in the glistening waves
                              underneath the glowing sun.

Jack Knill (11)
Bishopston Primary School

Love

What colour is it?
Love is the colour of strawberry ice cream, fresh from the freezer.
What does it smell of?
A chocolate cake, fresh from the oven.
What does it sound like?
When you hear your heartbeat when you see his or her face.
What does it taste like?
A sour sweet dissolving in your mouth.
What does it look like?
The smile on somebody's face when they are in love.
What does it feel like?
Warm water running down your spine.
What does it remind you of?
A big red heart, floating through the sky.

Rachael Davies (9)
Bishopston Primary School

14

Joy

What does it look like?
Families playing with each other with smiles on their faces.
What does it remind you of?
Playing in the field with the wind blowing in your hair.
What does it feel like?
It feels like a blast of joy up your body
And your cheeks aching with laughter.
What does it sound like?
Children giggling in the sun
With the waves splashing in the background.
What does it smell of?
Sausages cooking on the barbecue
With my feet buried in the sand.
What colour is it?
Joy is pale blue, like the pretty sea
And me playing with my family.

Katie Stein (9)
Bishopston Primary School

Love

What colour is it?
The colour of love is red like the sunset fading away into the sky.
What does it smell of?
Love smells of fresh roses.
What does it sound like?
Love sounds like walking into a misty morning going to school.
What does it taste like?
Love tastes of lovely fresh chocolate roses.
What does it look like?
Love looks like a big heart with three roses on top.
What does it feel like?
It feels very soft.
What does it remind you of?
Hearts and roses.

Morgan Israel (9)
Bishopston Primary School

Said And Done

Fear is like the dark black, midnight sky in the night,
Happiness is pink for children flying their kite,
Fear tastes like horrid things on your lips,
Happiness tastes like sweet sugar dips!
Fear reminds me of horrid things,
Happiness reminds me of peacocks
Spreading big graceful wings,
Fear smells like rotten food,
Happiness smells like sweet-smelling food
Being eaten by a dude!
Fear sounds like a ghost in your room,
Happiness sounds like cheering to the bride and groom,
As you can see, changing senses one by one,
Now all is said and all is done!

Alice Peters (10)
Bishopston Primary School

Fun

What colour is it?
Fun is the colour of a tent when we go camping.
What does it smell of?
Fun smells of a freshly cut piece of grass.
What does it sound like?
Fun sounds like a camera snapping on a good holiday.
What does it taste like?
Fun tastes like a 99 flake.
What does it look like?
Fun looks like everyone around me.
What does it feel like?
Fun feels like the wind rushing through my hair.
What does it remind you of?
Getting tickled by my brother.

Eve Clee (9)
Bishopston Primary School

Joy

What does it look like?
Joy looks like snow on a new winter day.
What colour is it?
Joy is orange like the oranges.
What does it taste like?
It tastes like strawberries as sweet as can be.
What does it remind me of?
Joy reminds me of Christmas when I get all my presents.
What does it sound like?
Joy sounds like the wind as it passes me at full speed.
What does it feel like?
Joy feels like the water of the sea.
What does it smell of?
Joy smells like the grass which we roll down.

Ieuan Hosgood (8)
Bishopston Primary School

Happiness

The colour of happiness is the colour of blue in a happy place.
What does it smell of?
Happiness smells of a warm fudge cake on a plate in front of me.
What does it sound like?
Happiness sounds like kids screaming and having fun.
What does it taste of?
It tastes of a lovely slice of pizza.
What does it look like?
It looks like people jumping into a warm swimming pool.
What does it feel like?
My friend and I playing football for Bishopstone.
What does it remind you of?
Happiness reminds me of going to the beach.

Cameron Rees Wishart (10)
Bishopston Primary School

Love

What colour is it?
Love is the colour of red!
Like lava trickling through your spine.
What does it smell of?
Roses! Freshly picked from a bramble bush!
What does it sound like?
The crunch of your winter boots crunching in the snow.
What does it taste like?
It tastes like a sweet, fresh from a sweet tree!
What does it look like?
It looks like a wave crashing on a rock!
What does it feel like?
Like your heart has exploded!

Olivia Adams (9)
Bishopston Primary School

Noise

Noise is red, like a rock band playing.
Noise is waves darkly crashing on the rocks.
Noise is grey for the sound of the wind
Blowing frantically on a stormy night.
It looks like guitars pounding on the stage,
Vibrating with every beat.
Noise is big, filling my ears.

Harry Knill (11)
Bishopston Primary School

Love

Love is red like the lovely dawning sun.
Love tastes like candyfloss melting in my mouth.
Love smells like beautiful red roses.
Love feels like a cosy blanket wrapped round you.

Callum Carson (10)
Bishopston Primary School

Sadness

Sadness is the black colour you get inside your head.
Sadness sounds like the song the grasshoppers sing.
Sadness looks like the scared look on an abandoned child's face.
Sadness reminds me of bad memories swirling through my head.
It feels like sadness blows up my head.
Sadness tastes like the salty sea crashing upon me.
Sadness smells of an open forest on a dark day.

Cara Silvey (9)
Bishopston Primary School

My Senses Poem Of Fear

Fear is black like the dark night,
Like the colour of a black pen,
Fear tastes horrid,
Gives people butterflies in their stomachs,
Fear smells like blood in the wars and fights,
And fear looks like scary stuff,
And spooky things.

Jack William Bates (10)
Bishopston Primary School

Courage

Courage is the colour gold, like a first place trophy.
Courage smells of freshly cut grass when I am running across it.
Swansea scoring the winning goal.
The pizza man making all the pizzas I eat.
It looks like courage to face up to your big brother.
A tickle down my spine.
It reminds me of the people who went to war for their country.

Samuel Stewart (8)
Bishopston Primary School

Joy

Joy is orange like the colour of oranges.
Joy looks like having fun on the playground.
Joy sounds like white clouds passing me when I am in the car.
Joy reminds me of surfing in the blue sea.
Joy smells like having a big chocolate cake on my birthday.
Joy feels like playing snowballs in the snow with my friends.
Joy tastes like a bright yellow banana.

Shaun Neale (8)
Bishopston Primary School

Joy

Joy is the colour of Smarties.
Joy is the sound of a car revving.
Joy looks like the sun.
Joy reminds me of putting my toes in the sand.
Joy smells of a sticky toffee apple.
Joy tastes like chocolate.
Joy feels like melting chocolate.

Eben Owen-Goodchild (10)
Bishopston Primary School

Fun

Fun is the colour of the blue sea going slowly.
Fun smells like a rose in the air.
Fun sounds like fireworks.
Fun tastes like marshmallows.
Fun looks like fireworks exploding.
Fun feels like the green grass.
Fun reminds me about my brother.

Bruce Killian (9)
Bishopston Primary School

Fun

Fun is the colour of the blue sky at night.
Fun smells of my birthday cake.
Fun sounds like rain dropping on my hands.
Fun tastes like chocolate cake in my mouth.
Fun looks like me playing in a pool.
Fun feels like me and my friends on the beach.
Fun reminds me of eating a cake.

Emily Irvine (10)
Bishopston Primary School

Anger

Anger is red like the flames in the fire,
Anger makes me feel like I'm mortal,
Anger tastes like flaming burnt sausages,
Anger reminds me of Hell,
Anger sounds like the Devil screaming,
Anger smells like burning toast,
Anger looks like the Devil ripping people's heads off.

William Brunnock & Tom Jenkins (9)
Bishopston Primary School

Anger

Anger is red like a box full of monstrosity trying to get out.
Anger sounds like a wolf howl of rage.
Anger smells of fire burning and smoke blowing up and up.
Anger feels like a volcano erupting.
Anger reminds me of hitting, pushing, shoving, don't do it,
Don't be like me.
Think, before you act.

Isabel Barclay (10)
Bishopston Primary School

Fear

Fear is black, like burglars creeping in the night.
Fear is red, like a big flashing red flame.
Fear is blue, like the deep, dark sea,
And fear is green like different kinds of creatures in the grass.
Fear is cold and freezing, like icicles in the winter.
Fear tastes horrid, like something bitter in your mouth.

Frazer Samuel (10)
Bishopston Primary School

Fear

Fear is something we don't understand
Something we don't like too,
Fear is something that lurks in our bedroom at night,
Which scares me a lot too.
It's hard to say what it feels like,
But I know you've felt it too.

Rhiannon Lloyd (10)
Bishopston Primary School

Sadness

Sadness is like a storm
Raging through a village
Sadness is grey like a rain cloud
Pouring water down on everything below
Sadness sounds like a baby's cry
Sadness is like a flame inside you.

Oliver Siddall (9)
Bishopston Primary School

Anger

Anger is red like the flames in a fire.
Anger tastes hot like a fresh baked pizza.
Anger reminds me of Hell.
Anger makes me feel like death.
Anger looks like the Devil's face.
Anger smells like the Devil's feet.

Alex Ibrahim (9)
Bishopston Primary School

Fun

Red is the colour of fun
It smells of apple
It sounds very noisy
And it tastes like strawberries
Fun is happy and soft
And reminds me of parties.

Flynn Ramsden (9)
Bishopston Primary School

Death

Death is brown, like a coffin with rotting bones.
Death is black, like a shadow that is hidden in bones.
Death sounds like little rats scurrying on the bodies
under tombstones.
Death feels like the force from a bullet that has just been fired.

Dafydd Griffiths (9)
Bishopston Primary School

Happiness

Happiness is white, like the colour of snow,
it feels soft and cold.
Happiness smells like a Christmas turkey,
it tastes like mint choc chip.
Happiness looks like presents in your Christmas stocking.

William David Lucas (10)
Bishopston Primary School

Sadness

What does it look like?
Sadness looks like sad faces.
What does it remind you of?
Sadness reminds me of people in my family,
that I haven't seen for a while.
What colour is it?
Sadness is the colour of dark blue.
What does it feel like?
Sadness feels like a broken heart.
What does it smell of?
Sadness smells of a dead rat.
What does it taste like?
Sadness tastes like disgusting medicine.
What does it sound like?
Sadness sounds like a violin playing.

Joseph Dowley (8)
Blaengwrach Primary School

Silence

What colour is silence?
Silence is the colour white, like plain paper.
What does it look like?
Silence looks like people around a table with unhappy faces.
What does it sound like?
Silence sounds like a clock ticking.
What does it smell of?
Silence smells of the cold air.
What does it remind you of?
Silence reminds me of cold, dark winters.
What does it taste like?
Silence tastes of a dry mouth.
What does it feel like?
Silence feels like you are really bored.

Ffion Davies (8)
Blaengwrach Primary School

Fear

What does it smell of?
Fear smells like a house on fire.
What colour is it?
Fear is an orange volcano.
What does it sound like?
Fear sounds like water rushing through big grey rocks.
What does it taste like?
Fear tastes like burning sauce in your mouth.
What does it feel like?
Fear feels like someone hitting you.
What does it remind you of?
Fear reminds me of people being mean to me.
What does it look like?
Fear looks like your mother shouting at you.

Alannah Horgan-Evans (8)
Blaengwrach Primary School

Love

What does it smell of?
Love smells of freshly grown scented daffodils.
What colour is it?
Love is the colour of bright red roses.
What does it look like?
Love looks like a bundle of red ribbons.
What does it taste like?
Love tastes like loveheart candy.
What does it remind you of?
Love reminds me of my mother and father when they first met.
What does it sound like?
Love sounds like birds singing in the trees.
What does it feel like?
Love feels like one hundred bumping hearts.

Shiana-Leigh Mackie (9)
Blaengwrach Primary School

Love

What does it look like?
Love looks like red hearts.
What does it taste like?
Love tastes like red, juicy strawberries.
What does it smell of?
Love smells of yellow daffodils.
What does it sound like?
Love sounds like birds singing in the trees.
What does it remind you of?
Love reminds me of seeing someone I haven't seen for ages.
What does it feel like?
Love feels like rose petals.
What colour is it?
Love is a pink heart.

Benjamin Burke (9)
Blaengwrach Primary School

Happiness

What does it remind you of?
Happiness reminds me of playing rugby.
What does it sound like?
Happiness sounds like birds singing in the trees.
What does it taste like?
Happiness tastes like a cooked dinner.
What does it smell of?
Happiness smells of delicious cakes.
What does it feel like?
Happiness feels like a warm blanket.
What does it look like?
Happiness looks like people dancing on the streets.
What colour is it?
Happiness is a red colour.

Thomas Jones (8)
Blaengwrach Primary School

Silence

What does it sound like?
Silence is the sound of a ticking clock.
What colour is it?
Silence is the colour of a blank piece of paper.
What does it remind you of?
Silence reminds you of a power cut in your house.
What does it smell of?
Silence smells of cold, frosty air.
What does it taste like?
Silence tastes like a flavourless ice cream.
What does it feel like?
Silence feels like a leather sofa.
What does it look like?
Silence looks like a vast white carpet.

Levi Slocombe (8)
Blaengwrach Primary School

Happiness

What does it look like?
Happiness looks like one million smiley faces.
What does it feel like?
Happiness feels like a giant hug from my mum.
What colour is it?
Happiness is the colour of the great big yellow sun.
What does it smell of?
Happiness smells of fresh baked toffee cookies out of the oven.
What does it remind you of?
Happiness reminds me of my sledge in the winter snow.
What does it sound like?
Happiness sounds like birds singing a smooth song.

Elliot Pavett (9)
Blaengwrach Primary School

Happiness Is . . .

Happiness is going on holiday to Spain.
Happiness is having a new rabbit to play with.
Happiness is a sunny day on the beach.
Happiness is being loved by your parents.
Happiness is having a birthday.

Happiness is having a new baby sister.
Happiness is having lots of money to spend.
Happiness is having full marks in a test.
Happiness is a never-ending school day.
Happiness is owning KFC.

Happiness is having lots of sweets to eat.
Happiness is sleeping over at your friend's.
Happiness is having a turkey dinner.
Happiness is having no homework to do.
Happiness is winning one thousand pounds.

Evan Richard Ward (9)
Bryncethin Primary School

The Writer Of This Poem

(Based on 'The Writer of this Poem' by Roger McGough)

The writer of this poem is . . .
As noisy as a ringing bell,
As tall as Big Ben,
As cold as an iceberg,
As large as a red hen.

As frozen as a statue,
As wild as a fierce lion,
As loud as a doorbell,
As steaming as a silver iron.

As mad as a crazy scientist,
As heavy as a house,
As crazy as a kangaroo,
As still as a mouse.

As dark as a black horse,
As loopy as a witch's cat,
As silly as a scarecrow,
As hard as a cricket bat.

The writer of this poem you see,
Is the one and only . . . me!

Callum Cooper (10)
Bryncethin Primary School

Horse

It's big
And has hooves
You can ride it and it can
Walk, trot, canter, gallop
It lives in a field
It will eat grass, apples
Carrots and drink water
It will walk, trot, gallop and canter.

Rosie Jones-Walker (8)
Bryncethin Primary School

The Writer Of This Poem
(Based on 'The Writer of this Poem' by Roger McGough)

The writer of this poem is . . .
As fast as a speeding rocket,
As hard as a rusty iron,
As funny as a wonderful comedian,
As heavy as a large lion!

As mighty as all the saints put together,
As tall as the BFG,
As weird as a creepy ghost,
As friendly as can be.

As scary as a man-eating wolf,
As wet as a tiny pebble,
As dull as a hairy donkey,
As hot as a steaming kettle.

As powerful as the dark universe,
As cool as the summer's breeze,
As brilliant as God,
As cool as can be.

The writer of this poem you see
Is the one, and only . . . me!

Jack Laidler (11)
Bryncethin Primary School

Hedgehog, Prickly, Spiky, Cool

Spiky, prickly, snuffling black nose.
Curls into a ball.
The hedgehog moves slowly, eating slugs, snails and worms.
They will live anywhere they want to,
Bushes or piles of leaves.
Prickling their predators, smelling for food.
Creeping along at night, they stick to the shadows.
Brown and grey, with black feet.

Mollie Hurley (8)
Bryncethin Primary School

The Writer Of This Poem
(Based on 'The Writer of this Poem' by Roger McGough)

The writer of this poem is . . .
As young as a newborn baby
As angry as a bee after a bear stole his honey
As tall as Mount Everest's peak
As fast as a crazy bunny

As rich as a leprechaun at the end of the rainbow
As loud as the motorway at night
As dumb as a rusted post
As wild as an unarmoured knight

As funny as a medieval jester
As imaginative as a cardboard box
As cheesy as Red Leicester
As sneaky as a bushy-tailed fox

As useless as a ripped-up piece of paper
As magical as a unicorn's horn
As bright as the Northern Lights
As green as my neighbour's lawn

The writer of this poem you see
Is the one and only . . . me!

Ben King (11)
Bryncethin Primary School

Fox

Long, thick, furry, rusty-red, bushy tail.
Cunning, sly,
Clever, bright eyes.
He's furry, he is a hunter and a chaser.
He's a poacher.
He's a stealer, tracker.
He's very fast.
He lives in a dark forest.

Tia Lewis (8)
Bryncethin Primary School

31

The Writer Of This Poem

(Based on 'The Writer of this Poem' by Roger McGough)

The writer of this poem . . . is
As smart as a 1000 page dictionary
as blonde as a yellow chick
as loud as a screaming firework
As short as a candlewick

As red as burning fire
As cool as you can get
As funny as a chuckling monkey
As wide as a jumbo jet

As slippery as fish
As slow as a hedgehog
As mad as a kicking bull
As heavy as an oak tree log

As fearless as a ferocious lion
As dangerous as a backfiring gun
As happy as can be
As marvellous as the sparkling sun

The writer of this poem, you see
Is the one and only . . . me!

Ieuan Jordan Hart (10)
Bryncethin Primary School

Zebra

Is it white with black stripes
Or is it black with white stripes?
Dash! It bolts really fast
And when it sees a lion, it dashes away.
It has brown eyes. Bashful, coy, modest,
Nervous, reserved. Feeling alarm,
Wait, watch, look, see, wait, watch,
Look, see.

Shauna Richards (8)
Bryncethin Primary School

The Writer Of This Poem
(Based on 'The Writer of this Poem' by Roger McGough)

The writer of this poem is . . .
As loud as the Big Bang
As cute as a tiny kitten
As fast as a speeding bullet
As soft as a winter kitten

As skinny as a brown twig
As clumsy as a blind bat
As clumsy as a dancing clown
As smelly as a disgusting rat

As wicked as a cold robber
As sly as the best spy
As pink as a shaved kitten
As yummy as a blueberry pie

As sporty as a rugby player
As jumpy as a spotty frog
As light as a piece of card
As lazy as a decrepit dog.

The writer of this poem you see
Is the one and only . . . me!

Tristan Jamie Baker (10)
Bryncethin Primary School

Friendship Is Everything

Friendship is a kitten playing with a ball of wool, the fun playing
with my friend.
Friendship is purple, the purple of my best friend's dress.
Friendship is the sun, giving me warmth.
Friendship is a daisy, fighting to survive on a windy day.
Friendship is beautiful, like a shiny diamond on a brand new
wedding ring.
Friendship is a dream, with us flying away into the distance.

Carys Penny (9)
Bryncethin Primary School

The Writer Of This Poem
(Based on 'The Writer of this Poem' by Roger McGough)

The writer of this poem is . . .
As loud as a black thundercloud
As small as a bumblebee
As brown as a huge crown
As weak as a small flea

As cute as a little bug
As light as a black and white kite
As soft as a fluffy rug
As hard as a great white shark's bite

As fast as a Citroen C4 rally car
As funny as a bouncing cat
As tasty as a Mars bar
As happy as a flying bat

As playful as a little rabbit
As tired as a sleepy dog
As hard as I try to give up a bad habit
As wet as a soggy bog

The writer of this poem you see
Is the one and only . . . me!

Nicholas Morgan (10)
Bryncethin Primary School

Love Is . . .

Love is sweet smelling roses in the flowerpot.
Love is the blue sea roaring at me.
Love is an orange, tasty fruit in the tree.
Love is a pink, fluffy cloud in the sky.
Love is a cream pillow as soft as can be.
Love is yellow, like wet daisies.

      Love is . . .

Bethany Elliott (7)
Bryncethin Primary School

The Writer Of This Poem
(Based on 'The Writer of this Poem' by Roger McGough)

The writer of this poem is . . .
As light as an empty box
As small as a rat's brain
As hot as a spicy chilli
As thick as a horse's mane

As cool as the Earth's breeze
As ridiculous as the king's joker
As funny as a stand-up comedian
As addictive as Coca Cola

As hairy as an adult baboon
As smelly as an underground sewer
As crazy as a box of frogs
As wild as horse manure

As skinny as a snooker cue
As gross as gone-off milk
As strong as a wild boar
As soft as a piece of silk

The writer of this poem you see
Is the one and only . . . me!

Ben Thomas (10)
Bryncethin Primary School

Untitled

Parrots in the rainforest killed
For food, captured to be pets.

Years ago, 11% of the world's surface
Was covered by rainforest
Now it is only 1%!
The rainforest is destroyed
At a rate of one acre every one second.

Courtney Pengilly (10)
Bryncethin Primary School

The Writer Of This Poem
(Based on 'The Writer of this Poem' by Roger McGough)

The writer of this poem is . . .
As quick as a blink
As bright as a shining light
As dangerous as a bare knuckle fight
As brave as a dark knight

As light as an inflated balloon
As cool as a spring breeze
As stupid as a buffoon
As noisy as buzzing bees

As cute as a fluffy puppy
As clean as a polished door
As clever as a thick dictionary
As sharp as a workman's saw

As thin as a brown twig
As rosy as Rudolph's nose
As hard as a horse's hoof
As sharp as witches' toes

The writer of this poem you see
Is the one and only . . . me!

Casey Sonnekus (11)
Bryncethin Primary School

Monkey

A monkey
Talks, he chatters,
He dangles from trees.
He climbs trees too.
He eats bananas,
He likes swinging on vines,
A monkey lives in trees.

Emilie Elizabeth Ward (8)
Bryncethin Primary School

The Writer Of This Poem
(Based on 'The Writer of this Poem' by Roger McGough)

The writer of this poem is . . .
As noisy as a musical fair,
As cute as a baby chick,
As cold as the swishing sea,
As thick as a hard brick.

As pretty as a bunch of roses,
As clean as the mopped floor,
As sporty as a leaping leopard,
As loud as a slamming door.

As soft as fluffy cotton wool,
As light as a floating feather,
As fun as a clown's party,
As smooth as brown leather.

As cheeky as a spoilt child,
As bright as a shining lighthouse,
As fierce as an Italian gangster,
As squeaky as an annoying mouse.

The writer of this poem you see
Is the one and only . . . me!

Elle-May Walters (11)
Bryncethin Primary School

Sea Lions

My secret animal feels slippery,
It lives in the lake, it eats fish and it likes to sunbathe in the sun.
If you are in a boat you may see one,
It likes to follow boats and it likes to balance a ball on its nose.
When it sees people, the animal sploshes
And it makes you wet and drippy.
Can you guess what it is?

Tamzin Beach (8)
Bryncethin Primary School

The Writer Of This Poem

(Based on 'The Writer of this Poem' by Roger McGough)

The writer of this poem is . . .
As smart as a lively dolphin
As cool as an icy pool
As quiet as a secret whisper
As sparkly as a jewel

As lazy as a sleeping sloth
Eyes as blue as the still ocean
As bossy as an angry goose
As slow as slow motion

As sweet as Cadbury's chocolate
As kind as a caring nurse
As fun as a joyous dog
As scary as a mummy's curse

As daydreamy as a cloud
As plain as a house brick
As wild as a bucking horse
As crazy as a rock and roll chick

The writer of this poem you see
Is the one and only . . . me!

Sophie Griffiths (10)
Bryncethin Primary School

Friendship

Friendship is like a guinea pig, making me laugh and giggle.
Friendship is like the colour white, sometimes feelings destroy it.
Friendship is dream time, when I dream I could fly.
Friendship is a carriage, with horses' shoes hitting the ground.
Friendship is the smell of sweets, I always want it.
Friendship is a magic wand that casts spells.
Friendship is a rose, that is growing all the time.

Emily Curnock (9)
Bryncethin Primary School

The Writer Of This Poem
(Based on 'The Writer of this Poem' by Roger McGough)

The writer of this poem is . . .
As fast as a bowling ball
As fun to play with as a baby's rattle
As cool as a winter breeze
As strong as a lion in battle

As kind as a dove
Hair as spiky as a hedgehog
As quick as a needle can weave
As fat as a wild hog

As brave as a soldier in World War II
As heavy as a blue whale
As funny as an insane comedian
As handsome as a sculpture and as pale

As pretty as a gleaming white daisy
Hair as thick as a horse's mane
As lazy as a green caterpillar
Eyes as brown as an old wooden train

The writer of this poem you see
Is the one and only . . . me!

Liam Smalldon (10)
Bryncethin Primary School

Love Is . . .

Love is red, like the smell of sweet strawberries.
Love is blue, like the sound of the waves calling me.
Love is brown, like the taste of toffee crunching in my mouth.
Love is yellow, like the look of the sun shining very bright.
Love is gold, like a one pound coin smooth on the top and bottom.
        Love is . . .

Jamie Sparkes (7)
Bryncethin Primary School

The Writer Of This Poem

(Based on 'The Writer of this Poem' by Roger McGough)

The writer of this poem is . . .
As sweet as a luxury chocolate
As quick as an incredible superhero
As loopy as a mad clown
But with marks never as low as zero

As active as a hunting lion
As smooth as a soaring bird
As smart as an award-winning dolphin
As strong as a fierce wildebeest herd

As explosive as an atomic bomb
As mysterious as an enchanting willow tree
As powerful as the British army
And as bright as a glowing key

As cool as the refreshing winter breeze
As tasty as a fresh steak bake
As tall as a large jungle tree
And as luscious as a ready-made chocolate cake

The writer of this poem you see
Is the one and only . . . me!

Stuart Young (10)
Bryncethin Primary School

Bat

The night hunter
He sleeps all day, he is awake all night
He hunts for creatures, he hunts all night with little fright
He flies around until
The sun is awake
Then he hides.

Dylan Evans (8)
Bryncethin Primary School

The Writer Of This Poem
(Based on 'The Writer of this Poem' by Roger McGough)

The writer of this poem is . . .
As blonde as a yellow chick
As quiet as a dormouse
As sweet as white sugar
As small as an ant's house

As light as tissue paper
As weak as a broken bone
As lively as a growing plant
As dead as a stone

As wicked as a cool gangster
As cute as a puppy dog
As colourful as the fascinating rainbow
As jumpy as a noisy frog

As skinny as a stick insect
As clumsy as a blind cat
As loud as a banging drum
As soft as a nice fluffy mat

The writer of this poem you see
Is the one and only . . . me!

Jodie Evans (11)
Bryncethin Primary School

Flying Squirrel

They are soft and brown.
They come out at night.
They are scared when they see people.
They make a noise.
They have a long bushy tail
And big whiskers.

Morgan Paget (8)
Bryncethin Primary School

The Writer Of This Poem
(Based on 'The Writer of this Poem' by Roger McGough)

The writer of this poem is . . .
As putrid as a vicious pirate
As marvellous as a magic trick
As weird as the world's weather
As ugly as a pile of sick

As heavy as a herd of elephants
As vile as a dragon's breath
As dull as a grey donkey
As quiet as death

As imaginative as a fairy tale
As sharp as a gladiator's spear
As bright as the golden sun
As rickety as a wooden pier

As hairy as a black gorilla
As fast as a wild deer
As tall as the Eiffel Tower
As sad as a trickling tear

The writer of this poem you see
Is the one and only . . . me!

Owen Jones (10)
Bryncethin Primary School

Love Is . . .

Love is the purple lavender smell in my garden.
Love is the brown horses neighing in the field.
Love is the pink strawberry gum taste in my mouth.
Love is the white new lamb looking at us.
Love is the black cat's fur, smooth in my hand.
　　　Love is . . .

Marie Eleanor Veasey (7)
Bryncethin Primary School

Happiness Is . . .

Happiness is love from your family.
Happiness is having as many wishes as you want.
Happiness is buying a big, patchy, cuddly rabbit.
Happiness is the stars so bright.
Happiness is the waves crashing on the shore.

Happiness is going on holiday to a warm place.
Happiness is racing on sports day, coming first.
Happiness is having big golden trophies.
Happiness is a book that never ends.
Happiness is having a big birthday party.

Happiness is poppies blowing in the wind.
Happiness is watching wildlife creeping around you.
Happiness is learning to do something new.
Happiness is playing with my closest friends.
Happiness is riding horses.

Megan Nicholas (9)
Bryncethin Primary School

Labrador

When it barks, it is loud.
It likes to eat meat.
It likes you.
It likes to eat.
It goes for a walk.
Dogs are mammals.
It likes you so bad.
They are full of beans.
When you have food they follow you.
They like you to death.
They are so fluffy.
I feel like I can talk to someone.
They like to eat some chicken.
Some can be nasty.

Chloe Elizabeth Jones
Bryncethin Primary School

Happiness Is . . .

Happiness is a sunny day
Happiness is playing with your friends
Happiness is a new baby
Happiness is going to the cinema
Happiness is a new baby crying.

Happiness is eating your favourite food
Happiness is seeing flowers in a field
Happiness is a new pet
Happiness is going on holidays
Happiness is having a birthday.

Happiness is the wind blowing in your face
Happiness is spending time with family
Happiness is a never-ending holiday
Happiness is Liverpool to win every match
Happiness is a river flowing.

Owen Hart (9)
Bryncethin Primary School

Winter

I love the winter
With all the leaves on the ground
I love the winter
Where all the golden colours can be found.

I love the winter
With blankets of thick white snow
I love the winter
With my rosy cheeks aglow.

I love the winter
You can make lots of fun
I love the winter
But I still love the sun.

Nathan Harris (8)
Bryncethin Primary School

Remember Me, Remember Me

Remember me, remember me,
You were sitting in front of me,
You were wearing silk black shoes and milky-green socks.

Remember me, remember me,
You were sitting in front of me, you seemed pretty happy,
Not pretty sad and you were not mad.

Remember me, remember me,
You were sitting in front of me,
You had silky brown hair and not very knotty,
Although it was pretty floppy.

Tia Miller (10)
Bryncethin Primary School

Happiness Is . . .

Happiness is having a cuddly pet.
Happiness is a never-ending holiday.
Happiness is a cry of a newborn baby.
Happiness is having a club to go to.
Happiness is having a fun birthday.

Happiness is spending time with your family.
Happiness is seeing flowers glistening in a field.
Happiness is eating your favourite food.
Happiness is having a new house.
Happiness is a sunny day.

Lowri Lester (8)
Bryncethin Primary School

Happiness Is . . .

Happiness is seeing stars shining in the night
Happiness is playing in the snow
Happiness is being full of love and joy
Happiness is a sunny day, so you can sit outside
Happiness is going on holiday.

Happiness is winning a million pounds in bingo
Happiness is playing with my dog in the garden
Happiness is winning in a competition
Happiness is having your spelling right
Happiness is reading library books.

Luke Cole James Brazell (9)
Bryncethin Primary School

Happiness Is . . .

Happiness is owning Smythe's.
Happiness is going to the cinema.
Happiness is having a rich family.
Happiness is having a robot.
Happiness is having a spaceship.

Happiness is ruling the world.
Happiness is a never-ending holiday.
Happiness is a never-ending book.
Happiness is having superpowers.
Happiness is being able to time-travel.

Rhodri Ellis (8)
Bryncethin Primary School

Monkey Madness

Humour is a monkey swinging from tree to tree,
he is happy.
Humour is blue,
the colour of a sunny day.
Humour is chocolate,
making you mad and sometimes crazy.
Humour is laughter,
it spreads to each other.
Humour is the forest trees,
the monkey enjoys the smell.

Chloe Olds (9)
Bryncethin Primary School

Happiness

Happiness is a horse in a meadow
Galloping towards you with joy,
Happiness is the sound of a stream
Flowing, making me calm,
Happiness is a fresh smell on a crisp morning,
Happiness is a beautiful meadow
Full of green grass,
Happiness is a home-cooked meal
Just come out of the oven
Making me feel warm.

Iwan Veasey (10)
Bryncethin Primary School

Black Rat

They creep silently.
They live in barns and rubbish bins.
They have lived for hundreds of years.
Sin, vices, malice, wickedness.

Ethan Connett-White (8)
Bryncethin Primary School

Tiger Happiness

Happiness is a flute playing its best music
Happiness smells like red roses that have just opened
Happiness is a baby tiger sleeping on the rocks

Happiness is the colour of red roses that have been grown
Happiness is bacon sizzling in a frying pan
Happiness looks like red roses growing out of seeds
Happiness is good people

Happiness looks like cheerfulness floating in the sky peacefully
Happiness is cheering from an audience.

Olivia Corbett (9)
Bryncethin Primary School

Happiness

Happiness is playing with my friends.
Happiness is leaving school.
Happiness is not working in school.
Happiness is catching a fish.
Happiness is doing maths.

Happiness is going on holiday.
Happiness is going fishing.
Happiness is a Sunday.
Happiness is getting all my spellings right.

Ryan Morgan (10)
Bryncethin Primary School

Love

Love is a baby puppy,. a baby puppy full of friendship
Love is a red rose, as red as my heart
Love is a kitten waiting for attention
Love is a puppy barking for food, needing to feed on feelings
Love is a chocolate cake, just baked, warm and sweet.

Charlie Thomas (9)
Bryncethin Primary School

Happiness Is Everything

Happiness is nice and caring
Happiness is a big friendship
Happiness is a big chocolate bar sharing it around
Happiness is a big cruise on a ship
Happiness is a big dinner
Happiness is an indestructible heart
Happiness is a hot bowl of soup
Happiness is a big bubble bath
Happiness is a big sign of friendship.

Aaron Jones (9)
Bryncethin Primary School

Love Is . . .

Love is pink, like a sweet-smelling flower.
Love is black, like the blackbirds that sing in the garden.
Love is brown, like a toffee treat that melts in your mouth.
Love is an orange sunset that fades away.
Love is like a cuddly teddy on my bed.
  Love is . . .

Isobel Longthorn (7)
Bryncethin Primary School

Love Is . . .

Love is orange, like the smell of oranges.
Love is white, like the seagulls singing in the air.
Love is green, like the taste of apples.
Love is red, like the roses looking at us from the ground.
Love is white, like the feeling of a human's skin.
Love is . . .

Liam Karl Svensen (7)
Bryncethin Primary School

Love Is . . .

Love is red, like the sweet smell of roses in your garden.
Love is cream, like a baby lamb calling its mum.
Love is pink, like bubblegum popping in your mouth.
Love is yellow, like a sunset slowly going down.
Love is brown, like a rusty old coin in my hand.
        Love is . . .

Mia Griffiths (8)
Bryncethin Primary School

Happiness Is . . .

Happiness is yellow, like a sweet-smelling daffodil.
Happiness is an Orange mobile phone ringing so loud.
Happiness is a pink piece of candyfloss tasting so sweet.
Happiness is a turquoise dress, sparkling at a ball.
Happiness is gold, like a slimy fish scale.
        Happiness is . . .

Brianna Kidd (7)
Bryncethin Primary School

Love Is . . .

Love is pink roses smelling sweet.
Love is the sound of green grass waving.
Love is orange, like the taste of a sweet fruit.
Love is looking at the ocean.
Love is a brown teddy bear feeling soft.
        Love is . . .

Emily Cutter (7)
Bryncethin Primary School

Love Is . . .

Love is red like sweet-smelling roses.
Love is the sound of bluebirds singing in the air.
Love tastes like orange tangerines.
Love is a brown slithery snail on my hand.
Love looks like a black midnight sky.
        Love is . . .

Hannah Morgan (8)
Bryncethin Primary School

Love

Love is a crying kitten.
Love is a red rose.
Love is the smell of ruby-red fresh roses.
Love is giving flowers to show your relationship.
Love is the freshest red strawberries in the land.

Kate Rogers (9)
Bryncethin Primary School

Loneliness

Loneliness is a bird twittering in the sky with no friends to hear.
Loneliness is black because it is sad.
Loneliness is a broken heart.
Loneliness is eating on your own.
Loneliness is people playing music and leaving me out.

Katie Norris (11)
Bryncethin Primary School

How To Make An Elephant

He needs . . .
a head like a rubber tyre
body like a bar of steel
eyes like a round ball
trunk like a long rope
mouth like a dark cave
jaws as strong as metal
teeth like sharp needles
ears like wings
legs like a strong piece of wood
tail like a long piece of string
and skin like the bark of a tree.

Corey Farrell (9)
Cwm Glas Primary School

Joy

It's as cute as a kitten
It looks as warm as a summer's day
It's as pink as tulips
It smells like hot dogs
It sounds like children running in a field
It tastes like ice cream
It reminds me of my dog wagging its tail
And licking its paws.

Katie Cooper (8)
Cwm Glas Primary School

Motorbiker

The colour is red like fire
The season is summer
The place is the countryside
The weather is sunny
The clothes are a red and blue leather suit
The furniture is a motorbike
The TV show is Top Gear
He eats chicken nuggets and chips.

Tia Stone (7)
Cwm Glas Primary School

A Clown

He is multicoloured.
The season is summer.
The place is a circus.
The weather is sunshine.
He wears a big hat with a flower that squirts out water.
The furniture is a stage in a tent.
The TV show is 'Clown World'.
He throws cream pies.

Holly Cooper (7)
Cwm Glas Primary School

Clown

It's the colour of a rainbow.
The season is summer.
The place is a blue and white circus tent.
The weather is a sunny day.
The clothing is a red rose and a wig.
The furniture is a penny farthing.
The TV show is Homer Simpson as a clown.
The food is a hot dog, dripping with red sauce.

Caitlin Williams (8)
Cwm Glas Primary School

53

Singer

She is the colour of red and gold
The season is a hot, summer's day
She performs in a studio of buttons
She is a sunny day
She wears a big, pretty costume
She sits on a golden chair
She is on X Factor
She eats party food to celebrate.

Georgia May Slee (7)
Cwm Glas Primary School

Despair

It feels like all rain clouds have come
It feels like the sun has gone
It's the colour of grey concrete
It smells of black smoke
It sounds like someone in pain
It tastes like onions
It reminds me of Mum shouting at me.

Nikhil Patel (8)
Cwm Glas Primary School

Joy

Joy feels like a heart of fun.
Joy looks like a roller coaster of love.
Joy smells of fresh candyfloss from the fair.
Joy sounds like children just come back from the park.
Joy tastes like bubblegum from the shop.
It reminds me of my hamster, he was as brown as chocolate.
Joy is as loud as a horse.

Finlay Hughes (8)
Cwm Glas Primary School

Happiness

It feels like a soft pillow.
It looks like the sun has brightened up.
It sounds like children playing in the park.
It tastes like orange jelly.
It's as yellow as the sun.
It reminds me of eating pizza.
It smells like ice cream.

Nathan Brooks (7)
Cwm Glas Primary School

How To Make A Guinea Pig

He needs ears like a knife
He needs paws like a needle
He needs eyes like a black cloud
He needs a nose like a tunnel
He needs whiskers like straws
He needs fur like wool
And teeth like pins.

Daniel James (7)
Cwm Glas Primary School

Joy

It feels like a fluffy quilt.
It looks like a warm joyful day.
It's as pink as a rose.
It smells of tasty candyfloss.
It sounds like a kitten's purr.
It tastes like lollipops.
It reminds me of my baby sister.

Shauna Curry (8)
Cwm Glas Primary School

Jealousy

It looks like pressure building up inside me, and my face going red
It feels like I just want to burst
It is the colour of fire spreading across the room
It smells like smoke surrounding me
It sounds like a constant roaring in my ears
It tastes as sour as vinegar
It reminds me of when I burst my sister's ball.

Callie Sullivan (8)
Cwm Glas Primary School

Happiness

It feels like hugging someone.
It looks like a smile on someone's face.
It is pink as candyfloss.
It smells like strawberries.
It sounds like laughter.
It tastes like sweets.
It reminds me of when I'm playing with my friends.

Katryn Wilson (8)
Cwm Glas Primary School

How To Make A Horse

She needs a brown or white body like a cushion,
Ears like devil horns,
A nose like brown chocolate,
Feet like a round tyre
And a tail like a girl's ponytail.

Chloe Cullen (7)
Cwm Glas Primary School

Two Terrible Twins

The basilisk is a fierce beast, it'll turn you into stone,
But if it's feeling hungry, it'll eat you, flesh and bone.
It has razor teeth and a killer stare,
If you meet it, please beware.
Its poisonous fangs will kill in hours
And it's the size of two big towers.
But don't forget its terrible twin,
The hydra, if you fight it, it will always win.
It's got many heads, immortal and mortal,
And if it sees you, you would not chortle.
It's got many heads and a spiked tail,
If you saw it you would quail.
But no one has found them, not even one,
No one has seen them, underneath the sun.

Adam Roynon (10)
Greenhill Primary School

Silent Love

Our love is silent and no one shall know
Now don't say a word, or you'll have to go
I will miss you so much, so keep your words steady
I have some words to say when you're ready
I will treasure you forever and ever and ever
And never forget you, never, never
So listen to my words, you know I'll promise
And the least I can do is give you a kiss
But anyway, there's no need to worry
Come on now dear, we'll have to hurry
Our love is silent, now don't spill a bean
But may I say you're the most handsome man I've seen
We're meant to be together, you know it's true
You know why I know, because I love you.

Rebekah May Davies (9)
Greenhill Primary School

Sophie's Song

There once was a pixie named Sophie Song.
She had a wonderful voice,
She sang all day long.
She sang in happiness, she sang in sorrow.
She sang in Fairy and Pixie Hollow.
But one day she had to make a choice,
A choice to give up her wonderful voice,
For her beloved sister was ill.
She grabbed her paper and quill
And wrote to her sister, 'I will.'
So in that land from that day on,
No one ever heard Sophie singing her song.

Megan Jayne Price (10)
Greenhill Primary School

Love

Love is the sound of bluebirds singing
And it's the sound of church bells ringing
Love reminds me of a big fluffy bunny
And it reminds me of sweet, sweet honey
Love's the taste of candyfloss
And it's the taste of cherry lipgloss
Love is soft, it's warm and cosy
Even sometimes it can be nosy
Love looks like a big red heart
But breaks when we're apart.

Courtney Williams (9)
Greenhill Primary School

Fairy-Tale Land

I once had a dream of a fairy-tale land
Where the butterflies made a beat for the band.
The sky was purple not like our own.
Where monkeys were kings and ruled the blue throne.
The ladybirds hopped on one leg in the sheds.
The chickens gave birth to pink eggs on their beds.
Where rabbits walked around with cat-like ears
And a tiger writes down whatever he hears.
Where the sun was small and fluffy and just out of reach.

Emily Wallen (10)
Greenhill Primary School

Tiger, Tiger

Tiger, tiger, you shine bright,
Glowing in front of the moonlight.
You go out hunting, you look so violent,
But deep down inside, you are quite silent.
I know why there's a tear in your eye,
I know why you're about to cry.
You look for shelter to keep dry,
You are saying your last bye-bye.
                Save the tiger!

Shane Pritchard (10)
Greenhill Primary School

Love

Love is red like a rose.
Love is sweet as sugar.
Love is a rose, pretty and bright.
Love sounds like a bunch of bells playing their tune.
Love looks like a bunch of tulips.
Love is a stranger that comes into your life.

Charlotte Forrest (8)
Greenhill Primary School

Love

Love is red and my boyfriend is named Fred.
Love smells like a rose, I love it when you wriggle your toes.
Love tastes like candy,
When I walk on the beach with you, it feels so sandy.
Love looks like hugs and kisses and when you're apart you miss it.
Love reminds you of friends and after a while, your friendship
never ends.

Ellie Jones (9)
Greenhill Primary School

Love

Love is red like a rose so sweet
Love tastes like candy so sweet to eat
Love smells like perfume so light
Love sounds like a heartbeat so tight
Love feels so soft and spongy like a bungee
Love looks like a Love Heart so lush
Love reminds me of nice people all in a rush.

Rebecca Brook (10)
Greenhill Primary School

Love

Love is red, the colour of two hearts meeting.
Love sounds like two hearts together beating.
Love tastes sweet like sugar.
Love feels safe and protective with each other side by side.
Love looks joyful and happy with two people laughing and joking.
Love reminds you of flowers in a flower bed, getting picked to go
with the wedding dress.

Shannon Forrest (8)
Greenhill Primary School

Love

Love is like pink bunches of flowers and some bells
                                    playing their tune.
Love is as sweet as sweets and candy.
Love is a friend but then the friendship ends.
Love is like wedding bells ringing from the church.

Emily Hough (7)
Greenhill Primary School

Fear

Fear is grey like a cloud on a rainy day.
Fear is like seeing Jeeper Creeper's peeper.
Fear is alone like you have no home.
Fear is quiet.
Fear is like a tidal wave and your mother telling you to behave.

Kristian Watkins (9)
Greenhill Primary School

Sunny Poem

The cats were fighting over food
and the sun looked down sadly.
The kids did their homework
and the sun looked down happily.
The cats shared the food
and the sun looked down happily.
The kids were being silly
and the sun looked down sadly.
The animals were dying because of pollution
and the sun looked down sadly.
The man was throwing litter
and the sun looked down sadly.
A woman was picking up the litter
and the sun looked down happily.

Sophia Melhas (8)
Pentrepoeth Junior School

Our World

More floods,
but still the sun shines down.
Animals dying,
but still the sun shines down.
Water being wasted,
but still the sun shines down.
Greenhouse gases are blocking the sun's light,
but still the sun shines down.
People drop trash,
but still the sun shines down.
People not recycling,
but still the sun shines down.
Goodnight.
Sleep tight.
Don't forget to turn off the lights!

Sam Dickerson (8)
Pentrepoeth Junior School

Poem

The children were sick
and the sun looked down sadly.
The birds sang
and the sun looked down happily.
The cans were recycled
and the sun looked down happily.
People were zooming in the shop
and the sun looked down happily.
The sea was splashing on the rocks
and the sun looked down happily.
Children were working hard in class
and the sun looked down happily.
The landfill site was full
and the sun looked down sadly.

Michelle Overment (7)
Pentrepoeth Junior School

Our Changing Planet

Animals and polar bears are dying,
but still the sun shines down.
People are not recycling,
but still the sun shines down.
Others are dropping litter,
but still the stars twinkle at night.
My neighbours aren't turning off the taps,
but still the stars twinkle at night.
Polar ice is melting,
but still the sun shines down.
Goodnight,
Sleep tight,
Don't forget to turn off your nightlight!

Luke Brannigan (7)
Pentrepoeth Junior School

What's Happening To Our World?

People waste water
But still the sun shines down.
Polar bears' ice is melting
But still the sun shines down.
People waste electricity
But still the stars twinkle at night.
People waste paper
But still the stars twinkle at night.
Habitats disappearing
But still the sun shines down.
People not recycling
But still the sun shines down.

Hollie Riley (8)
Pentrepoeth Junior School

All Around The World

The lady picked up the litter
and the sun looked down happily.
The rabbits ate orange carrots
and the sun looked down happily.
New leaves grew on the trees
and the sun looked down happily.
A man dropped litter on the beach
and the sun looked down sadly.
The autumn came and the leaves fell off the trees
and the sun looked down sadly.
The rabbits had no food because the crops failed
and the sun looked down sadly.

Abigail Sinnott (8)
Pentrepoeth Junior School

Save The Earth

People cutting down the trees
but still the stars twinkle at night.
People wasting food
but still the sun shines down.
People wasting electricity
but still the sun shines down.
People not recycling
but still the sun shines down.
People are wasting heat
but still the stars twinkle at night.
Please think what you are doing
and let's not lose the eco fight!

Jordana Jones (7)
Pentrepoeth Junior School

Pony Land

The pony ran through a stream
and the sun looked down happily.
Some babies were swimming
and the sun looked down happily.
Friends played football
and the sun looked down happily.
It was Easter
and the sun looked down happily.
At Easter nobody got presents
and the sun looked down sadly.

Joseph McFetrich (8)
Pentrepoeth Junior School

Poem

The children ignored the teacher
and the sun looked down sadly.
The puppies played with their new toy
and the sun looked down happily.
The little boy had lost his favourite toy
and the sun looked down sadly.
The children were ill
and the sun looked down sadly.
The rugby team won
and the sun looked down happily.

Jude King (8)
Pentrepoeth Junior School

Poem

The sea swayed
and the sun looked down happily.
People threw rubbish in the sea
and the sun shone down sadly.

Scott Lewis (8)
Pentrepoeth Junior School

The Sun In Our Sky

The butterflies flew around the people's heads
and the sun looked down happily.
The small boy pushed a toy bus
and the sun looked down happily.
The children were licking ice cream
and the sun looked down happily.
The library was so quiet
and the sun looked down happily.
The people had rain
and the sun looked down happily.

Faris Massrojih (8)
Pentrepoeth Junior School

The Sun Looked Down

The fox ran around the tree
and the sun looked down happily.
The dog ran to his owner
and the sun looked down happily.
The children played chase
and the sun looked down happily.
The children played up
and the sun looked down sadly.
The sea swayed calmly
and the sun looked down happily.

Keira Martin (9)
Pentrepoeth Junior School

The Sun Looked Down At The Children Playing

The children built sandcastles
and the sun looked down happily.
A ship crashed into rocks
and the sun looked down sadly.
The children played outside
and the sun looked down happily.
The flower died
and the sun looked down sadly.

Adam Hooper (7)
Pentrepoeth Junior School

Seashore

The sea swayed
and the sun looked down happily.
The boats bobbed up and down on the sea
and the sun looked down happily.
A fox was eating a chicken
and the stars looked down sadly.
A fox was fighting
and the sun looked down sadly.

Lewis Cook (7)
Pentrepoeth Junior School

67

What Does The Sun See?

The flowers grew
and the sun looked down happily.
The flowers started to die
and the sun looked down sadly.
The stream swayed side to side
and the sun looked down happily.
The stream got too rough
and the sun looked down sadly.

Ethan Rees (8)
Pentrepoeth Junior School

Sad Poem

The whales got caught up in the plastic bags
and the sun looked down sadly.
The people were polluting the world by throwing rubbish on the floor
and the sun looked down sadly.
The lions were fighting over meat
and the sun looked down sadly.
The tornado hit the house and destroyed it
and the sun looked down sadly.

Kian Jones (8)
Pentrepoeth Junior School

Poem

The sea was rough and the pirates were attacking
and the sun looked down sadly.
The animals in the zoo went mad
and the sun looked down sadly.
The children in school were playing happily
and the sun looked down happily.
The man was riding his bike and he fell off
and the sun looked down sadly.

Callum Howard (8)
Pentrepoeth Junior School

Stars

The children played with their ball
and the sun looked down happily.
The children lost their ball
and the sun looked down sadly.
The dog found the ball
and the sun looked down happily.
The children were ill
and the sun looked down sadly.

Phoebe Connor (8)
Pentrepoeth Junior School

Heart Poem

Father Christmas gave presents to all the children
and the stars looked down happily.
The children went to bed quietly
and the stars looked down happily.
Butterflies were flying around the trees
and the sun looked down happily.
The children played with the ball
and the sun looked down happily.

Demi James (8)
Pentrepoeth Junior School

The Sun

The man was riding his bike
and the sun looked down happily.
The boy went to the fair and he twisted his ankle
and the sun looked down sadly.
The Antarctic was melting
and the sun looked down sadly.
The cars were going past on the motorway
and the sun looked down happily.

Dafydd Peters (8)
Pentrepoeth Junior School

Animals

Animals
Care for us, we care for them,
Soft as snow,
Cuddle and warm, we take them through it all,
Pigs eat anything,
Horses with courses, apples and all,
Hot, cold or smelly,
Jumping, crawling, running, playing and more,
Outdoors or inside,
They live happily forever more.

Katie Samuel (8)
Penygawsi Primary School

Snow

Snow,
Falling softly,
Twinkling, dropping proudly,
Sparkling like ice flakes,
Soft as a teddy bear,
Cold as your hand,
As gentle as staying still,
Chilly.

Ffion Morgan (8)
Penygawsi Primary School

Celts

Celts,
Humiliated Romans,
A deafening scream,
As naked as a rock,
Proud of themselves
Strong!

Kieran Smith (8)
Penygawsi Primary School

Springtime

The sky is blue and the grass is green
And while the birds twitter,
The golden sun shines down like crystals
And the smell of flowers smells like roses.
Trees slowly shake hello,
Flowers go *nod, nod*
And now the day is over,
It is time to say bye-bye.

Amy Louise Olding (9)
Penygawsi Primary School

Autumn Leaves

The leaves in autumn are happy and bright
Their hair is rain
They wear a covering of soft white snow
They eat the sap from the trees
Their breath is warm and snug
The leaves' children are the nuts from next door
They long to become red, yellow or bright
The leaves' enemy is the gale of the wind.

Daniel Maclean-Howell (8)
Penygawsi Primary School

Water

Water,
Smashing waves against the rock,
Roaring sound of crashing waves,
Water helps plants grow,
Crashing! Bashing!
Like transparent rain,
Wet, soggy, cold.

Abbie Prosser (9)
Penygawsi Primary School

Rain

Rain
Splashing, pouring
Dripping, splattering noises
Wet like teardrops
Puts smiles on frogs' faces
Sensational!

Sophie Price (9)
Penygawsi Primary School

Puppies

Puppies
Play happily
Bark all day
Cute like pretty kittens
Proud to have them here
Delightful.

Elizabeth Anna Samuel (8)
Penygawsi Primary School

Gods

Gods
Beat anything
Sound, deafening roar
Like nothing seen before
You feel so, so scared
Unstoppable.

Daniel John Jones (9)
Penygawsi Primary School

Water

Water,
Sprays gently,
Drip-drop sounds,
Crystal-like cold diamonds,
Ice-cold frozen shower,
Relief.

Anais Fripp (8)
Penygawsi Primary School

Snow

Snow
Falling softly
Twinkling, sparkling, dropping
Just like sparkling drops
It feels frosty, ice-cold
Chilled.

Sophie James (9)
Penygawsi Primary School

Love

Love
Brings together,
Magical, enchanted, pretty,
Lovely, like a toffee apple,
Like cherryade, fizzy and mad
Gorgeous.

Yasmin Tyler Howells (9)
Penygawsi Primary School

Snow

Snow,
Freezy flow,
Fun to go,
Crystal-like icy wind,
Cold, shivery, silvery like diamonds,
Freeze!

Melissa Cayford (8)
Penygawsi Primary School

Tyrannosaurus

Tyrannosaurus,
Eats meat,
Its deafening roar,
Massive like skyscrapers,
My knees wobble with fright.
Colossal.

Liam Tan (9)
Penygawsi Primary School

Bang

Jumps along,
Chug, chug, bang,
It likes chugging along,
It feels like a bomb,
Bang!

Joel Davies (9)
Penygawsi Primary School

Chef

Chefs cook
Sizzle, crackle, bang
Just like lava popping
Hot, sweaty, greasy, oily
Bang!

Connor Robertson (9)
Penygawsi Primary School

Hawks

Hawks
Glide high,
Squawking, noisily screech,
I would feel very scared,
Predator.

Lewis Weeks (9)
Penygawsi Primary School

My Dog

Colour as lovely as a shiny red rose.
Teeth as sharp as a million blades.
Feet as small as my hand.
Tail as short as a little mouse.
Nose as wet as the heavy rain.
Mouth as wide as a laptop opening up.
Eyes as blue as the sparkly sea.
Ears as small as a small, sticky glue stick.
Claws as sharp as a vampire's teeth.

Amber Gilbert (10)
St Nicholas CW Primary School, Cardiff

The McCoy Cake

Ingredients:
5 swigs of Conor's amazing golfing.
8 pinches of Kurtis' fantastic boxing.
10 pinches of Netty's fast cleaning.
4 Welsh rugby matches for Ian.
2 tips of Cathy's tasty gravy.
1 beep of Dennis' huge yacht.
100 massive smiles of Zoe.

Method:
Get one enormous pot and set it at 250°.
Pour Cathy's gravy in very slowly.
Tip in some of Netty's fast cleaning.
Chuck Conor's amazing golf moves in.
Drop Kurtis' fantastic boxing moves in.
Then crunch in Dennis' huge yacht.
Finally sprinkle Ian's Welsh rugby matches.
Grate Zoe's massive smiles
And then serve it up to family, *mmm!*

Zoe McCoy (9)
St Nicholas CW Primary School, Cardiff

Cardiff Blues

Tito smashes through the players like a rhino.
Halfpenny speeding to the try line like a cheetah.
Blair kicks like a horse.
Molateka growling towards the other player like a lion.

Rushy controls the game like a hungry T-rex.
Roberts dances through the air like the fastest bird.
Shanks slithering through the grass like a snake.
Williams slices the players like a shark.

Tehya Lee (10)
St Nicholas CW Primary School, Cardiff

Emotion Poem

Wonder
Wonder is a beautiful sunrise glowing elegantly,
It tastes so sugary and sweet, like sweets,
It sounds like birds chirping, the sounds of Heaven,
It smells so lovely and delicious, like fresh brownies,
It feels so funny like a newborn puppy,
It looks like Heaven in a golden paradise.
Wonder reminds me of all my great memories.

Horror
Horror is a terrifying wolf hunting human prey,
It tastes like rotten eggs and dead apples,
It sounds like deadly screams from everywhere,
It smells rotten and dead,
It feels shattered and sharp,
It looks old, dead and horrifying,
Horror reminds me of my worst nightmare.

Lukas Wallis (10)
St Nicholas CW Primary School, Cardiff

Cardiff Blues Metaphor

Tito munching through the opposition defence.
Leigh Halfpenny diving madly for the try line.
Ben Blair's kick slicing the right post.
Martin Williams stealing the opposition's ball.

His shoulder shattered under a crunching tackle,
Shanklin galloping down the right wing for a lethal try.
Andy Powell grabbing the ball.
Gethin Jenkins goes in for a vicious tackle.

Niall Routledge (10)
St Nicholas CW Primary School, Cardiff

77

The Man United Pie

Ingredients:
2oz of munching tackles.
4 teaspoons full of spectacular passes.
2 shaking goalposts.
A sprinkle of yellow cards.
Ronaldo's special red card.
10oz of referees.

Method:
Sprinkle 2oz of munching tackles into a pot.
Throw in a pinch of yellow cards and cook for 4 mins until you hear,
'That's an evil foul!'
Then stir with a spoon until you can hear the final whistle.
For the finishing touch, add Ronaldo's special red card
and 10ozs of referees.
Then sit back, relax and enjoy your pie!

Liam McNamara (11)
St Nicholas CW Primary School, Cardiff

I Am Me!

I am me
I have green eyes
I have long hair
I like dogs
I hate snakes
I am good at swimming
I am friendly
I am me!

Livvey Wadsworth (7)
St Nicholas CW Primary School, Cardiff

I Am Me!

I am me
I have blue eyes
I have long hair
I like Halle and Isobel
I hate cats
I am good at drawing
I am Halle's friend
I am me!

Olivia Savage (7)
St Nicholas CW Primary School, Cardiff

I Am Me!

I am me
I have an earring
I like maths
I hate selfish people
I am good at football
I am Khalid's best friend.

I am me!

Mason Parsons (8)
St Nicholas CW Primary School, Cardiff

My Horse

Colour like chocolate brown.
Hooves sharp as a nail.
Mouth as big as the River Severn.
Eyes like a buzzing fly.
Ears like a car wheel.
Tail like a long rope.
Nose like a hook.

Alisha Cornish (9)
St Nicholas CW Primary School, Cardiff

I Am Me!

I have long hair
I have green eyes
I like my sister Isobel
I hate cats
I am good at drawing
I am Olivia's best friend
I am me!

Halle Cotterrall (7)
St Nicholas CW Primary School, Cardiff

I Am Me!

I have long hair
I have blue eyes
I like Ellie Donald
I hate being hit
I am Kelsea
I am me!

Kelsea Jenkins (7)
St Nicholas CW Primary School, Cardiff

Daydreaming

Floating across silent skies,
Being lazy, I close my eyes.
Drifting further overland,
Falling gently on golden sand.
Palm trees swaying side to side,
Bouncing waves on an incoming tide.
Voices carried upon the air,
A colourful sun setting somewhere.
Noises wake me, I open my eyes,
Then I suddenly realise . . .
        I'm daydreaming!

Emily Taylor (10)
Ton-Yr-Ywen Primary School

The Bored Girl, Lilly

There once was a girl called Lilly
She liked to go to the park to get chilly
Every day she used to come out and play
But now she's always bored in the house all day.
Then her mother told her to get out and play
Instead of being bored in the house all day.
So she said, 'No way!
I want to be bored in the house all day.'
So her mother said, 'Get out and play
Otherwise you will be grounded,
And then you will be bored in the house all day.'
So she said, 'Fine then.'
So she knocked on her friend called Sizzle.
She said, 'Will you come out and play?'
But Sizzle just slammed the door
And said, 'Just go away!'
So Lilly said, 'Fine then.'
And it was the end of the day.

Holly Brain (10)
Ton-Yr-Ywen Primary School

Hip Hip Hog

There once was a frog called
Hip Hip Hog,
Who liked to sit on a little log,

He hipped and hopped and hipped and hopped,
Right up to the big treetop,

He looked around and thought, *oh my!*
It was forbidden to go up this high,

He felt himself slipping and slipping,
And that was the end of his little living.

Megan Jones (11)
Ton-Yr-Ywen Primary School

81

I Don't Want To

I don't want to go swimming
I don't want to go on a stroll
I want to go snowboarding
in the North Pole

I don't want to play rugby
I don't want to play catch
I want to play football
and sew up my patch

I don't want to eat pancakes
I don't want to eat flies
I want to eat snails
while dipping them in pies!

I don't want to climb a ladder
I don't want to climb a tree
I want to climb a mountain
dressed as a bumblebee.

Sarah Butler (10)
Ton-Yr-Ywen Primary School

The Spooky Scream Of Hallowe'en!

I walk around in the autumn sky,
so many figures passing by.
With my pumpkin pot with me,
I look around at what I can see.
The spooky figures stare at me, wondering
what I'm supposed to be.
I hear a sound right by my feet. It was the
sound of
'Trick or treat?'

Noor Sobka (10)
Ton-Yr-Ywen Primary School

Polly And Her Dolly Called Molly

Polly loved her dolly called Molly
And went shopping with her friend Holly
She bought a really nice ice lolly
The flavour was lime
But Polly didn't realise the time
Until she heard the church bells chime
She realised she was late
She ran through the estate
To meet her mate
Her friend was still there
Holding her teddy bear with such care
They went to the park till it got dark
They walked home together
They were best friends forever
And always together.

Gabbie Thompson (10)
Ton-Yr-Ywen Primary School

A Good Dream

A good dream can make you fly
High as the moonlit sky.
It feels like a nice quiet lullaby,
In your pillow you gently sigh . . .
How high can you fly in the moonlit sky?
And how long is a nice quiet lullaby?
But it's what you feel like when they're through,
Tells you what you want to do!

Menna Poole (11)
Ton-Yr-Ywen Primary School

You'll Be Sorry If You Don't!

Once I saw a chocolate bar sitting by itself,
But then my sister said to me, 'Don't eat it by yourself,
Because you are so greedy you'll be sorry for your fate,
Because whose trousers are too tight, now they've put on weight?
Stop a moment, think awhile, your pupils are dilated,
For if you shared that treat with me, then I would be elated!'

Leila Navabi (10)
Ton-Yr-Ywen Primary School

The Piano

The piano
A true musical wonder
The keys collide with the sound
The feeling is an impeccable feeling
The piano.

Queena Lee (10)
Ton-Yr-Ywen Primary School

Haikus About Me

My name is Dewi
I live in Cardiff, Wales
I am eight years old

I like computers
My favourite colour's green
I'm very active

I live in Wales
I adore the Welsh country
We own Cardiff Bay

I have a white house
I love reading funny books
I have a puppy.

Dewi Rees (8)
Ysgol Melin Gruffydd

Colour Poem

Red!
Red is the sign of love
Red is burning fire
Red is falling lava
Red is the colour of blood

Blue!
Blue is the colour of the sea and sky
Blue is the colour of my eyes
Blue is the colour of my teddy bear's nose
Blue is the colour, peaceful and calm

Purple!
Purple is the colour of the purple grapes
Purple is the colour of a ballgown
Purple is the colour of a bruise

Green!
Green is the colour of grass
Green is the colour of an apple

Orange!
Orange is the passion of fruit
Orange are the autumn leaves
Orange is a colour of hair
Orange is a tiger.

Seren Murray (9)
Ysgol Melin Gruffydd

Colours

Pink is the colour of a fairy's dress,
Black is the colour of a great big mess!
Blue is the colour of water,
Purple is the colour of a dress a father bought his daughter,
Orange is the colour of a tangerine,
Turquoise is the colour of the big wide sea.

Megan Burt (10)
Ysgol Melin Gruffydd

Colour Poem

Red is for embarrassment,
And for love.
Orange is bouncy,
And for fun.
Yellow is for happiness,
And for joy.
Green is for peace,
And for calm.
Blue is for sadness,
And for cold.
Purple is confident,
And strong.
Pink is warm,
And snugly.
Grey is dull,
And down.
Brown is safe,
And friendly.
Black is scary,
And spooky.
All these feelings are inside us.

Chloe Burrage (8)
Ysgol Melin Gruffydd

Untitled

Red is for war
Red is for love
Red is for fire and for leaves
Red is for Wales
Red is for fire engines
Blue is for Man City
Red is for Cardiff Blues
Red is for hat
Red is for bag.

Sean Flynn (8)
Ysgol Melin Gruffydd

The Rainbow Poem

Pink is the colour of my face
Pink is the colour of my pillow

Blue is the sky
And blue seems sad like a willow

Green is the grass
Green is all slimy

Brown is chocolate
But brown can be grimy

Orange is an orange
Orange is fun

Yellow is bright
Yellow is the sun

Black is scary
Black is spooky

Purple is girly
Purple is kooky.

Seren Vincent (9)
Ysgol Melin Gruffydd

Colour Poem

Blue is the colour of the sky.
Blue means flying high.
Green is a tree, and it can be tea.
Red is anger, red is blood.
Brown is the colour of the dirty mud.
Pink is for hearts and warmth and love.
Yellow's the sun shining above.
Dark green for seaweed, under the sea.
Silver is the colour of the front door key.
Black is the cave which is spooky and dark.
Every colour of the rainbow gives off a bright spark.

Francesca Board (9)
Ysgol Melin Gruffydd

Magic

Gold is for treasure,
Pure, pure riches.
Gold is for magic,
Not for witches.

Silver is for the unicorn,
And Pegasus too.
Silver is for mist,
And the fairies near you.

But what is both colours,
All mixed together?
Lots of magic,
Mixed forever.

In the night,
Try wishing on a star,
You never know,
You might go far . . .

Georgina Morgan Savastano (8)
Ysgol Melin Gruffydd

Ten Colours

Green is groovy.
Black is gloomy.
Purple is calm.
Pink means you no harm.
Red is blood.
Brown is mud.
Yellow is bright.
Blue is the colour of my kite.
Grey is boring.
Orange is the colour of the morning.

Ten colours,
What do you like?

Megan Eckley (9)
Ysgol Melin Gruffydd

Untitled

Grey is gloomy
Purple is happy
Blue is calm
Peach is the colour of your palm

Orange is the colour of the fruit
Black is the colour of my suit
Green is the colour of the grass
Brown is the colour of dirty glass

Yellow is the colour of the sun
Light brown is the colour of a hot cross bun
Pink is the colour of ham
Red is the colour of jam.

These are all colours of the rainbow.

Megan Dugdale (9)
Ysgol Melin Gruffydd

Colour Crazy

Black is the colour of sadness
Red is the colour of madness
Blue is relaxing
Yellow is shining

Green is crazy
Grey is lazy
Orange is happy
White is the colour of your nappy

Turquoise is the colour of the sea
Gold is the colour of my key
Brown is the colour of the roots
Silver is the colour of flutes

Twelve colours, which is your favourite?

Beca Hayes (10)
Ysgol Melin Gruffydd

Colour Poem

Blue is the colour of the peaceful ocean.
Blue is a winter and chilly moment.

Yellow is the colour of the hot, bright sun.
Yellow is the sign of happy summer fun.

Pink is the colour of an old, tubby pig.
Pink is the colour of my aunty's new wig.

Green is the grass which is under my feet.
Green is the colour of the very tall trees.

Red, a strawberry, cherry and a rose.
Red, the colour of a clown's odd nose.

Orange, a word with which nothing rhymes,
Orange a fruit, but more importantly, a colour.

Angharad Rees (10)
Ysgol Melin Gruffydd

Colour Poem

Red is for anger.
Blue is for water.
All the colours
Are around us!
Black is for darkness.
Grey is for sadness.
All the colours
Are around us.
White is for doves.
Pink is for love.
All the colours
Are around us.
Look at all the colours
Around us!

Mali Bryant (9)
Ysgol Melin Gruffydd

Colour Poem

Green is the colour of trees swaying happily
with healthy lives.

Yellow is the colour of the sun,
skipping ropes and footballs
and children having fun.

Pink is the colour of spring,
children playing,
what a happy thing.

Red is the colour of rage,
Red is the colour of my hamster's cage.

Blue is the colour of the ocean
it fills our lives with a happy emotion.

Sara Jones (10)
Ysgol Melin Gruffydd

Colour Poems

Green is for grass
Growing in the garden.
Green is the beanstalk
That giants climb.
Green is the colour of trees
That are walking.

Blue is the colour of the sky
Up above.
Red's the colour of love
In the skies.
Red is also for anger,
But
That isn't too wise!

Miriam Singer (9)
Ysgol Melin Gruffydd

Untitled

Orange is for orange
Blue is for sky
Blue is for Man City
Red is for Man Utd
Red is for Liverpool
Red is for Arsenal
Brown is for chocolate
Yellow is for sun
Blue is for sea
Green is for grass
Pink is for sunset
Brown is for mud
Orange is for basketball.

George Bruce (8)
Ysgol Melin Gruffydd

Animal Haikus

Rabbit
Bouncing peacefully
Sees a cat, bounces away
Leaving cat behind.

Stag
Standing tall and proud
An animal approaches
Stag leaping away.

Fish
Swimming in the sea
He sees a shark, swims away
Moving fast and quick.

Harry Jones (10)
Ysgol Melin Gruffydd

Haikus

Jesus
The peace of the Earth
who willingly sacrificed
Himself for the Earth.

God
God is existence
Creator of the planet
the Light of the world.

The Devil
The Devil is death
The bane of all existence
the evil inside.

Twm Rowley (10)
Ysgol Melin Gruffydd

Colour Poem

Red is for heat but also for war
Red is for danger, like jamming your hand in a door

Blue is for sadness, like when you cry
Blue is for rain which comes from the sky

Yellow is for the sun which twinkles in space
Yellow is for the sand on the beach
I need to hurry to pack my case

Green is for the Christmas tree
Green is for the grass that I can see
Green is for leaves when summer comes
Green is for the leaves on a freshly ripened plum.

Lara Bryant (8)
Ysgol Melin Gruffydd

The Colours Of The Rainbow

Red:
Red is evil, like the Devil
And Hallowe'en!

Yellow:
Yellow is bright and colourful
Like the crown of the queen

Pink:
Pink is like flowers
Also like a pig!

White:
White is the colour of Top Gear's Stig!

Bethan Dew (9)
Ysgol Melin Gruffydd

Colours

Red is the passion of love.
Blue is the sky up above.
Yellow is sand, a boiling sun.
Brown is the colour of my chocolate bun.
Purple is the colour of foxgloves.
White is the colour of the doves.
Orange is the colour of a satsuma.
Black is the colour of a puma.
Green is the colour of the thick forest.
Pink is the favourite colour of every florist.
Multicoloured paints, oh, so fine
On a painting palette of mine!

Gruffudd Alun (11)
Ysgol Melin Gruffydd

The Multicolour Poem

Orange is the colour of fire,
Very light brown is the colour of a mouldy tyre,
Pink is the colour of your skin,
Grey is the colour of a tin,
Purple is the colour of the book that I'm reading,
Blue is the colour of a lovely ring,
Yellow is the colour of the sun,
Dark pink is the colour of my face when I run,
Green is the colour of a pear,
Black is the colour of a puma which is very rare,
Red is the colour of roses,
Brown is the colour of a door when it closes.

Georgia Garland (9)
Ysgol Melin Gruffydd

Untitled

Red is angry, fiery and hot
Red is love and red is blood
Orange is bouncy, juicy and fun
Orange is for the setting sun
Yellow is mellow, a day in summer
Yellow is bright like a banana
Green is evil, green is naughty
Green is growing stuff like cabbage
Blue is the colour of the deep blue sea
Blue is the colour of sky up above
Black is for darkness in the night
Black is for Hallowe'en, what a fright!

Carys Davies Jones
Ysgol Melin Gruffydd

Untitled

Red is a colour of blood.
Brown is a colour of mud.
Green is a colour of a pea.
Blue is the colour of the sea.
Orange is a colour of fruit.
Black is the colour of my boot.
Yellow is the colour of my hat.
Grey is the colour of a bat.
Colours are all around.
Wherever we are bound.

Lillie Phillips (9)
Ysgol Melin Gruffydd

Colour Poem

Blue is the colour of the sea and sky.
Red is the colour of fire.
Green is the colour of the beautiful green grass.
Purple is the feeling of fresh fruit.
Orange is the colour of me and you.
Blue is the feeling of drifting rain.
Red is the passion of love.
Green is the swaying trees up above.
Purple is the feeling of splodging paint.
Orange is a colour of a roaring tiger.

Lauren Williams (9)
Ysgol Melin Gruffydd

Orion's Gold Belt - Haiku

Orion's gold belt,
A constellation in space,
Is one of many.

Daniel Mallett (10)
Ysgol Melin Gruffydd

The Bird · Haikus

Flying through the sky
Is a bird looking for prey
Swooping in and out

Looking for his tea
He sees a cat on the wall
Cat runs away fast

But cat is too slow
Bird gets him around the neck
Cat is no longer!

Annie Bird (10)
Ysgol Melin Gruffydd

Colour

Clouds are white, as white as bread.
Brown is the colour of chocolate spread.

Gold is the colour of a ringing bell.
Red is the colour of devils in Hell.

Waterfalls are blue, they fall in lakes.
The hot yellow sun can make you bake!

Forests are green, as green as spring leaves.
Big green blades grow on palm trees.

Cian Moriarty (10)
Ysgol Melin Gruffydd

Colour Poem

Red is for danger, deep, deep danger.
Green is for understanding thoughts.
Blue is for tears and also for rain.
Orange is for sunset, nice, soothing sunset.
Brown is for cocoa beans that make chocolate, nice, nice chocolate.

Iestyn Jones (9)
Ysgol Melin Gruffydd

Untitled

Red is for danger.
Red is for Man Utd.
Red is for a red pen.
Red is for Liverpool.
Red is for Arsenal.
Red is for fire.
Red is for strawberries.
Red is for danger.
Red is for blood.

Morgan King (8)
Ysgol Melin Gruffydd

Colour

Green is as friendly to you and me.
Blue is subtle as the sky and sea.
Red is for roses when you go out for food.
Pink is a colour that will change your mood.
Orange is a sunset in the afternoon.
Peach is the colour of your skin, the sky's glow before we see
                                                    the moon.
Yellow is the sun, like the morning rise,
The world is as colourful as my family and friends!

Lili Powell (9)
Ysgol Melin Gruffydd

Colour

Red is the colour of fury and love.
Blue is for water and sky above.
Green is the colour of grass and leaves.
Brown is the colour of stalks on trees.
Gold is the colour of a necklace, jewellery.
Pale is the colour of a face giving mercy.

Jay Bowen (10)
Ysgol Melin Gruffydd

Rainbow Colours!

Red is the colour of love,
White is the colour of a dove,
Blue is the colour of above,
Pink is the colour of a pig,
Purple is the colour of my wig,
Orange is the colour of a tropical fruit,
Yellow is the colour of a lemon cake,
Every time I see a rainbow
I think of all these things!

Annie Marks (10)
Ysgol Melin Gruffydd

A World Of Colour

Green is the grass.
Blue is the sky.
Red is for danger, but I don't know why.
Yellow for happiness, laughter and smiles.
Orange for the sun, I can see it for miles.
Indigo and violet are just like each other.
They go well together like sister and brother.
A rainbow is so beautiful and bright.
What a shame you can't see it at night.

Laura Anderson (9)
Ysgol Melin Gruffydd

Colour Poem

Red is the colour of love,
Blue is the sky above,
Pink is a fairy's dress,
Black is the colour of my DS,
Green is the colour I play on every day,
Yellow is the colour of horses' hay.

Jack Turner (10)
Ysgol Melin Gruffydd

Untitled

Red is for love and anger and blood.
Yellow is for the sun.
Blue is for the ocean, the sky above,
Green is for the grass and the trees.
Brown is for the mud that's under the ground.
Pink is for a pig.
Purple is for a storm.
Grey is for clouds.
Orange is for oranges and a colour of a sunset.

Eve Jones-Moss (8)
Ysgol Melin Gruffydd

Untitled

Purple is calm, like the birds floating,
Gold is nice, like the bell going *ting,*
Pink is cool, like the colour in the rainbow,
Red is also a colour of the rainbow.
Orange is like the sun in the sky,
Yellow is like the colour of my hair dye,
Brown is like the mucky mud,
Silver is the colour of my school stud.

Sioned Broad (9)
Ysgol Melin Gruffydd

Haikus

Blue is the greatest
It's for Cardiff City's top
They are the greatest.

I love them the most
I go and watch them beat clubs
Blue is the Bluebirds.

Jake Chaletzos-Sealey (10)
Ysgol Melin Gruffydd

Rainbow Colours

Red is the colour of love,
White is the colour of a dove,
Blue is the colour of above,
Pink is the colour of a clean pig,
Purple is the colour of my wig,
Orange is the colour of a tropical fruit,
Yellow is the colour of my lemon cake,
When I see my rainbow I think of my poem.

Nia Phillips (10)
Ysgol Melin Gruffydd

Untitled

Orange is the colour of my tangerine,
Yellow is the colour of my tambourine,
Blue is the colour of the calm sea,
Green is the colour that won't harm me,
Pink is the colour of my flower bed,
Brown is the colour of the hair on my head,
Black is the colour of the embroidery on my coat,
Purple is the colour of the dots on my boat.

Elis Miller (9)
Ysgol Melin Gruffydd

Untitled

Red is the leaf, the shine of the sun.
Red is the colour of my heart.
Red is like an exploding volcano.
Red is like a fire truck.
Red is like a fire.
Red is like a beautiful rose.
Red is like a coloured pencil.
Red is like a pencil case.

Rhys Hatherill (10)
Ysgol Melin Gruffydd

Colour

Green is the grass that the wind blows,
Green is the jelly that wobbles to and fro.
Blue is the sky that we always see,
Blue is the bluebird, and he always sees me.
Red is the blood flowing through your body,
Red is the lava flowing through somebody.
Pink is the beauty of the woman he loves,
Pink are the clouds that set up above.

Ben Marshall (10)
Ysgol Melin Gruffydd

Untitled

Blue is funky.
Brown is like a monkey.
Pink is really fluffy.
Red is the colour of my sister when she's nutty.
Black is ugly, like love at first sight.
Yellow is the colour that caught my sight.

Six colours that I like!

Robyn Whitaker (9)
Ysgol Melin Gruffydd

Untitled

Red is the colour of evil.
Green is the colour of nature.
Yellow is the colour of the bright, bright sun.
Blue is the colour of the sky up high.
Purple is the colour of the little, purple lavender.
Orange is the colour of the fire in the lounge.

Beca Jones (9)
Ysgol Melin Gruffydd

The Man

That man likes jam
but he also eats ham
his feet are so smelly
you can smell them from the telly
his belly's so big, it wobbles like jelly.

Zach Headon (9)
Ysgol Melin Gruffydd

My Colours

Blue is for the deep, deep ocean.
Brown is for chocolate and mud.
Orange is for the light, light sunlight.
Red is for deep, deep danger.
Multicolour is for anything and everything in the world.

Ben Vesey (8)
Ysgol Melin Gruffydd

Love

Love feels like someone who gets you a bunch of flowers.
The colours of love pink and red, like some lovely cherries.
Love reminds me of a field of flowers.
When a boy gets you some sweets on Valentine's Day,
when a boy says he loves you.

Erin Moore (10)
Ysgol Mynydd Bychan

Loneliness

You feel deserted, all you see is grey.
You don't have anyone to play with, nothing is there to look at.
You feel sad always, you have time left.

Jonathon Faulkner Leworthy (9)
Ysgol Mynydd Bychan

Roller Coasters

Roller coasters are so fast,
it feels like your skin is peeling off!
If you're brave enough and all set,
get on and you will scream, I bet.

You will find them in theme parks
but rarely seen in fields and on grass.
Brave, scared, leap in a queue,
here are some theme parks to go to.

Oakwood, Busch Gardens, there are lots of flags,
There are two I know in Holland,
Duinrell, Efteling, these are the two,
Don't just lie about watching TV, get out there.

There are over a thousand colours for roller coasters
And over a million types.
It's a shame you have to travel the world
To get to them.

Johan Hoogendoorn (9)
Ysgol Mynydd Bychan

The Lost Bunny

Imagine being lost when you wanted to play,
Seeing lots of people and the sky is grey.
Poor little soul, sitting on a carpet of leaves,
Found a tree and fell asleep.
Then that night some people came around,
Then a little girl picked him up, now little bunny was lost, now found.

That night the sky was black,
Poor little Chester, no food to be found.
Chester lay calmly in his bed
Then fell asleep on his bed of warm snow.
'Come on then Chester, go with the flow,
Let's go for walkies in the cold snow.'

Megan Ware (9)
Ysgol Mynydd Bychan

Pets

I have a pet, fluffy and brown,
When I'm with him I'm never down,
He crawls along the floor
And creeps out of the door.

A pet is bright colours
Swirling in the sky,
A pet feels like joy on a summery day,
A pet sounds like the sea,
As gentle and calm as can be.

Tanisha Daley-Byard (9)
Ysgol Mynydd Bychan

Sport

Sport makes you feel tired and weak, at the same time
strong and energetic.
Its colour is the flaming red of tiredness and anger
to put those points on the board.
Sport reminds me of the flaming heat of Spain.
Sport has the taste of a gum shield on your teeth.
Sport sounds like the whistle of a ref and insane cheering
for their country.
It looks like balls flying and individuals moving at high speeds.

Asher Marc Johnson (9)
Ysgol Mynydd Bychan

Friendship

Friendship feels like you're on a ferry of companions
and you're on an island called Buddy Island.
The colour of friendship is rainbow colours.
Buddies remind me of happiness and joy to my mind
and make my fingers tingle.

Megan Millward (9)
Ysgol Mynydd Bychan

Animals

Animals feel furry and fluffy, smooth or slimy.
Animals are big or small, massive or tiny.
Animals are happy or sad, angry or playful.
Animals live in cages, live in houses.
Some might be in your downstairs cupboard!
Animals, animals need you to look after them,
Feed them, groom them,
But most of all they need you to love them!

Sophia Innocent (9)
Ysgol Mynydd Bychan

Love

When I see *love* I see a heart hovering
I see the colour of brightness and fun
The *love* is strong and kind
I feel it dancing and going round in joy
It's hard to find *love*
But you'll find it soon
I'm sure you will
By daylight or moon.

Lydia Gwen Ellis (9)
Ysgol Mynydd Bychan

The Snowstorm

A boy imagining the things he will see on the way
through the snowstorm.
A lonely traveller travelling in the snowstorm turns black
on the cold snow.
A traveller travelling in the snowstorm cannot find his way
in the white snow.
You can still hear the boy shouting, *'Help! Help!'*

Finn Dixon (9)
Ysgol Mynydd Bychan

Rugby Is . . .

Rugby is a sign of toughness, everyone keeps it real.
Everyone who plays is a block of steel.
Rugby is a risk that not many would take.
They always do something bad, so there are no people to boo.
Rugby's a challenge to tackle hard.

Jonathan Jeynes (9)
Ysgol Mynydd Bychan

Baking

Baking feels like you're in Heaven.
The colour of baking is light and crispy.
It reminds me of baking creamy cookies.
Baking is about fun.
Baking delicious cookies, cakes and Welsh cakes, of course.

Rhys Howarth-Lewis (9)
Ysgol Mynydd Bychan

Young Writers Information

We hope you have enjoyed reading this book - and that you will continue to enjoy it in the coming years.

If you like reading and writing poetry drop us a line, or give us a call, and we'll send you a free information pack.

Alternatively if you would like to order further copies of this book or any of our other titles, then please give us a call or log onto our website at www.youngwriters.co.uk.

Young Writers Information
Remus House
Coltsfoot Drive
Peterborough
PE2 9JX
(01733) 890066